D1375488

BRENT LIBRARIES
Please return/renew this item
by the last date shown.
Books may also be renewed by
phone or online.
Tel: 0115 929 3388
On-line **www.brent.gov.uk/libraryservice**

NOTE

The painting used as an image on the cover, 'Mountains of Hearts and Diamonds', by Stanley Greaves, was Martin Carter's favourite from the Hearts and Diamonds series from the 1980s.

THE POEMS MAN

Poems dedicated to Martin Carter,
true friend and respected mentor.

STANLEY GREAVES

PEEPAL TREE

First published in Great Britain in 2009
Peepal Tree Press Ltd
17 King's Avenue
Leeds LS6 1QS
UK

© Stanley Greaves 2009
Interview © Stewart Brown and Stanley Greaves

ISBN 13: 9781845230869

Supported by
ARTS COUNCIL
ENGLAND

CONTENTS

#1 POETRY

In the time of revised spells
when the language of poetry
is no more the tool of fools,
granite flowers will bloom
on the mountains, where
determined rivers flow
in furrows clawed by jaguars.

1978.

2# TO A POET M.C.

And the horses
And the drums,
the night does not still
dogs practising to howl.
With leaves stuck to feet
the condemned commit miseries
which even lilies in their hearts
cannot devotedly conceal.

The absence of truth
hoods the eagle's eyes,
angels cannot be heard,
only the warden of words
stringing poems,
as the precipitous wren
its galaxy of songs.

1979.

#3   FOREWORD

Two lines formed with words
spoken by Martin Carter, begin this poem.

"Your name is walking about
in a country of sprinting men."
The wordless meat of memory
is a vision mystery of encompassing
and the anxiety of a remembered curse.
Let the chessmen play!
The plural toe pads my solace,
and yet all around
unconscious slavering
nettles the skin into forgetting
the constituent assembly of humanity.

1981.

4# FAREWELL

Tree-tall friend
of a thousand conversations,
peace between us
has always transcended
known boundaries of arrogance,
seeking, with feeling born
in envelopes of concern,
that numinous domain
of cautious mysteries,
welcoming as the earth is
for every floating seed
on stairs of air and rain.
I remember a fellowship,
walking between adamant trees
with singing bottles
from indescribable points.
No longer now can I witness
your quotidian presence
like precarious trees
beside a forwarding river.
Memories like sharp shadows
create yet sharper image
from the blunt turmoil
of dumb separation.

1987.

5# TO MARTIN

Sadness and joy
a paradox of feeling,
of participating in
that special function,
the condition of friend.

1993.

6#   LAST SUPPER

Lone so far,
each word dropping
like corn
from elevated cob.
what is a poem,
but the main course
of some fabulous feast.
Poet – head of table,
visitors, guests
sampling each line
as succulent slice.
Applause becomes sauce,
each shining verse
accepted, digested,
becomes the centre
of yet another story
of yet another poem,
elsewhere.

1995.

7#   TIME   I

Wizened fruit
crumpled can
underfoot the poet,
ubiquitous witnesses
to the collapse of time.
In magical instance,
that dot in sky or sea
conversant with
his mote-in-eye,
becomes phantom craft
or painful poem.

Can poets claim sovereignty
within the house of time.

1996.

8# THE POET'S GATE

I boxed the face of the dog
with a book of poems.
It was more difficult
to deal with the gate
as with the poet's words,
dense intractable meanings
locked fast like kernels
in shells of hardest Brazil.
Between webs of words spoken
and rails of words written,
I sensed an enigmatic land
peopled by metric meteors.

Seated by his indulgent window,
I fitted his words between
leaves of listening balsam
like some fastidious carpenter,
wondering why today's relevance
is tomorrow's redundancy,
and why that dog is
still standing
at the gate.

1996.

9#   THE HERO

The hero steps
from his obvious shadow
into realms of the shadow.
The profoundest path
is made easy, like
walking on whispering shells.
What the foot knows
the mind now hears.
There is no horizon of limit,
fruits can fall upwards,
fingers challenge eyes
in the test of loving skin.

The stepping hero
loiters in metric maze
and disputes now
what he knew then.

He would not be hero,
but first stepping poet
of certified intent.

1996.

10#   MARTIN

And what do you think
of a voice that oft-times speaks
in lines of sheer poetry.
It seems a halting here,
a darting there, fish
or bird of relentless poignancy.
The wonderment of that word
plucked like honey/kernel
of intransigent flower/nut.
That flash and falling –
bright sudden meaning.
What do you think of
voices that now speak
in lines of sheer poetry.

1997.

11# THERE IS A POEM HERE

There is a poem here,
lines of layered meanings, and
surprises like twisted commas.
Object and dream become words,
words flex to symbols.
Rhythm, a net to trap souls
while symbols, just so, fly
in portentous conjunctions.
Dread accompanies meaning
and red silence follows
impatient marks on paper.

Eyeless in the night
ambition awaits the poet,
the poet, that sometime meaning
rising with delayed dawn.
There is a poem here.

1997.

12# THE LAST WALK

I write to you, I write to you
and so a plangent tale is born,
like old Cuffy, Atta, Akkara
and the fateful siege of Dageraad,
as Guyana now, enshrouded in
the curse of ballots of deceit.
In the very streets you walked
smoke and bullets seek victims
awaiting the elusive count, the way
young lovers and salient memories
haunt the grey adamant wall
that created a long haunted coast.

Oh parlous day! Oh parlous day!
The votive streets you often danced
stand strangely still and enchanted
like Chinese landscapes you loved.
In bye-ways, shadows absent themselves
as your being, now bereft of words,
is drawn by horses of wondrous form
worshipped in your cosmic visions.
The litany of priest and family, and
unfamiliar constraints of church,
even hymns must have seemed strange,
but not the songs of grace you loved –
"Where have all the flowers gone!"
of proclaimed and private triumph,
your family Wylde and far Ireland.

The gods of Parnassus, name place
like some ruined Guyana plantation,
must have in deliberation drawn
the ironic circle of chanting citizens
hurling political names in fury along

your last walk to a defined space,
fury often limned in adamant lines
living in your trenchant poems
refuting seasons of pernicious politics.

Sentinels of trees, salute of proud guns
greet you – "the poems man", borne
in a flag-draped boat of purple wood
riding a tide of true lucid poems
on that journey eternally defined by
welcoming Osiris in green and black
and Isis attending in robes of white
celebrating the truth of life and death –
a demanding mantle you proudly wore.
I write to you, I write to you, finally
and so a plangent tale is born.

1999.

#13.   THE POEM

Take time, take time,
statements made must last.
Vortex of words in metric feet
must never become
fictive plodding homilies
or grand deceptive allegories of self.

The wayward evergreen poet
with web-like magic
must snare bones and rainbows transforming them,
seeds of paradise fruits to poem trees.

1999.

14.   OVER AND AGAIN.

Flanked by two angels
I recited an ancient poem of events
starting and ending at the same place
and all over again.

Like the story of the seed
parched and forgotten
until expected rain,
the dream of becoming a tree
is now another dream.

On goes the poem of things
starting and ending all over
like birds to trees
or lightning to static wood.

1999.

15.   COCONUT – POEM.

Coconut water lives in shells
as poems the poet's mind.

As fibre binds shells
how are poems clothed.

Birds pick fruit
departing in song
and imaged thoughts
hanging like coconuts
fall into poetic consciousness.

2000.

#16.   WORD.

It is the time of thread and spade,
time to measure useless words
and bury them in the wind.
From every ancient trunk and cavern
visions will be extracted. Flawed concepts
however confined in world-of-books
must be discarded like cracked bricks.
Always the poet must taste
fine rum and sound of each constructed syllable
as dress of poems.
This is the time of thread and spade.

2000.

#17.   IMAGINARY LIFE.

I did not recognize it.
"...everything lies under your feet",
the Poems-man said.
Many leaves have fallen since.
It seems now,
as if I have always lived in
constructs of ageless imagination,
in dimensions oblivious of cultural boundaries.
It is here,
bright fruits are always sweet,
birds do not eat carrion,
crude extravagances never appear as rain.
It is all I ever wanted
in a midnight's minute.

2000.

#18.   NEW WORD.

Leaves,
a variety of twisted colours
clothe my friend the tree.
Shapes are born to my eye
before words name them,
posing intrusive questions
of precedence.
Each day's inevitable debate
between leaf and cloud
between spoon and sand
create new words,
and new words
incalculable events
in the poet's domain.

2000.

#19.   FLYING WORDS.

Bark of the dog
whose shadow has gone home
hits the wall like a stone.
The poet's visions are kept close
like the handle of a knife
or secret words that can fly.

God made an angel
who indulged in word-play,
so poets learnt to let words fly
through every careless crack
as dogs will bark,
and shadows walk.

2000.

#20.   THE MIRACLE.

There is a moment when
visions and words escape infinity
becoming object poem.
Believing ourselves protagonists
we are but vectors of that explosive miracle.

As snakes move into new skin
my friend the poems-man would say
"…we should be of that order"
 continuously divesting ourselves
of poems the miracle brings.

2000.

#21.   SAMENESS.

Late night glass
of small spiced rum,
companion book,
and convoluted memories,
seductive sleep intervened.
Steadfast floor restrained
a book's descent to infinity.

In early-rayed morning,
rum was still in glass,
book and memories splayed,
on foot- awakened floor..
I drank the rum,
was it same rum,
same book,
same memories,
same floor.

2000.

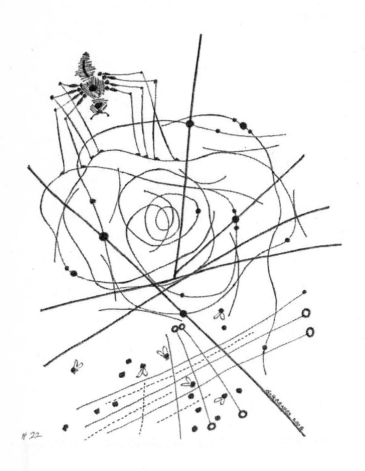

22

#22.   SPIDER AND FLY

Walking the metaphysical horizon
of poetical conceits,
the spider's agility patrols
webs of meditative traps.
Our mind's eager cunning
dances a willingness to deal with
angels and pins,
arguments blind and austere as
stones in every convenient river.
Meanings become curious flies
seeking holes in the web
defying its definition of space
as we do webs of existential perplexities.

2000.

#23.   DREAM OF DEMERARA

I have had a dream,
a dream relating to many others
of a land divided by a wall
and a city denying itself.
Street-children do not talk of politics,
the grey homeless never sing.
Streets have only memories of trees,
mad prophets laughed away in the sun
and poets known only to themselves.

I have had a dream,
a dream relating to many others
of a land divided by a wall.
Divided as the minds of a populace
dancing on shattered walls of reason.

2001

#24.   BANANA GROVE.

Hope of young leaves
fingered lazy clouds,
old leaves become earth.
A single plant becomes a grove,
as line after line
infinite plantations of poems.

Infinity remember,
is a certain distraction -
long shadows leaving a house,
actors finding the right roles,
a poet, significant words.

2001.

#25.   BIRTH OF WORDS.

Think of elapsed eons
before a word like "hence"
becomes a necessity.
It is neither thing nor event,
supportive shoes nor death of a friend.

Imagination imagined itself
demanding the word "hence"
to sugar temporal meanings,
as royal women everywhere
painted their eyes.

Power of a word created the universe.
as the ultimate intoxication of speech,
daring to expand meaning shouted
"hence…"

2001

#26.   POETIC CONCEITS.

Eagerly I used rare words
to create a new poem
and thought it fair
to visit a dictionary
which soon created
a field of despair.

Conceits of all manner
littered every page,
like exotic beasts on savannahs.
"jeremiad" and "picaresque",
 "sprezzatura", "zeugma",
and others quite rare
as "Clevelandism" to spare.

With eyes near blind
but not in disgrace
I saw the poem's title
had a revered place.
"Conceits Poetic" was my wish,
"So it is", the page announced
with open deliberate relish.

2001.

#27.   HOUSE AND ROAD.

He walked by
a complacent house,
proud bright.
Inside,
a welcoming inquisitive space,
as his mind
to poems brought by the wind.

Fire invaded the road,
house and poems lost in smoke
unlike creatures of free jungle trails
whose days, unlike roads
have no singular meaning.

He walked by
a smoking house
bright lit by burning poems.

2001.

#28.   THE POEMS-CAT.

Rug colours sang
as if time was listening.
Cat looked,
touched the supine book,
turned pages with its nose
and read Rumi's words.

What was written
was what poets did.
Any cat knows.

2001.

#29.   AWAKENED.

Have you ever been awakened
by a thought, not as
metaphor of enlightenment,
but brought from sleep
as bread from oven.

Here now,
robed twice in dream
and blessed thought
we rise as coloured marvel,
fish never before seen.

2001.

#30.   ADJECTIVES ADVERBS

Adjectives,
Adverbs,
handmaidens of poetic aesthetics,
dangerous
like legions primed for conflict
attacking prime states
Nouns – impervious minds,
Verbs – quietly stole.

Protection lies in poetic forms
like fortress walls where
each stone guards its position.
Adjectives,
Adverbs,
bane of visions
bane of life.

2001.

31

#31. BLUE CRAB.

The poet wrote
it was possible,
as any blue crab finding a hole
to discover "…truth of the world",
but unlike that lucky crab
and convenient hole
I have not found,
nor has the poet described
"…truth of the world".

2002.

#32.   QUIET HOUSE.

The house is quiet,
bats no longer drop fruit, obbligato
for my everlasting monologue.
I wish walls would speak
of ambitions and secret wishes
of outrageous dimensions,
that I could write them.

2002.

#33.   NOW.

The present cannot be measured.
How long is "now".
That we name dimensions
is just a construct to put wings to fear.
Yet must we live moments
giving form in poems
to perceptions arriving unannounced,
like pond-bottom bubbles
bursting in metaphysical haze.

2002.

#34.   WORDS. I

Like entities from that fabled box
delighting in sudden freedom,
words take just a moment
to say the unintentional,
even by a mind primed to write.

Conversations in spirit,
like the back of a hand,
present another word-scape
as monitor of poetic forms
against monstrous creations.

2002.

#35.   WORDS. II.

Words be dangerous, whether
from the mouth of the beloved
or cryptic marks on paper.
Comes one word on air
virtually nothing by itself,
but caught in context, like bird in a cage,
it becomes a sword of sound
ready to wound any heart.
Words be dangerous.

2002.

#36.   TIME.

I looked at his book,
"Selected Poems" it said.
Twenty eight years of friendship
need an image, so daily
I welcome as poems palm trees he loved
scarred trunks marking each fallen leaf
changing colour,
as poems each reading.

I recall when, in memoriam, images
becoming words would fall,
startling my fingers to write
what I would read long after,
wondering why the "I" that reads
is not the "I" that writes.

2003.

#37.   CONCEPT.

As through stone windows
of an ancient pyramid
sun-rays play upon my face.
I consider intimations,
giving them form,
as did priests of Egypt
making intangibles finite.

An ant will contemplate a rock,
a rock a cloud, and man,
verbal constellations
whose meanings emerge
in awakening minds.
as if dream-forms,

2003.

#38.   POEMS-BOOK.

I opened a familiar book
letting images create words,
as servant to image.
That is their history.
I read, smiled at
the sound of small success in words.
and winked at
the unwavering horizon of stars.
Ants with sparks of sand
can create hills
as my words hopefully
a poem.

2000.

#39.   PENS AND WORDS.

Pens and books sleep beside me.
Arising, I shake sheets
of a crop of dreams
they should have written.
My friend the poet once said
"You can write a poem on anything – if a poet".

The urge to write comes
like firefly's steady light as
I try to write a story
of pens and books beside me.

With ready pen, open page
I write of something else
instead of their mutual love.
How must I contrive then
to write of pens and books.

2003

#40. DREAMS AND POEMS.

What madness this
poems replacing dreams.
If this a dispensation
I accept the consequences
of every gift dream, every poem
as forest relates to seed.
To dream and poem what am I.

2003.

#41.   HANDS.

Flowers in a vase,
matches, blistered finger
but innocent flame.
What is the connection.

Like bats to orchard thoughts fly,
seductive as colours without form
urging fingers to write.

Poems do not have fingers,
they own mine.

2003.

#42. THE POEM.

Stop writing.
Pick up the mallet before
every wayward thought
demands to become-
a poem.

2003.

#43.   MEANING.

I consulted a word
found many meanings
relevant to ambitious events
like wholesome prizes.
I replaced the book.

Flight comes and disappears
with every bird. So
what do we know about flight,
meanings of words or
gesture replacing a book.

2003.

#44. FORM.

Forms are made,
wood, words
or whatever.
One eye of approval
caresses form,
the other conjures meanings
of the form of forms.

2003.

#45.   WORDS JUST SO.

Never a trick knitting words
to sponsor fair meanings,
that word and another – just so
perhaps without certain meanings
at the moment.

Read me spectacular lines,
Only the gifted mad can fathom.
"Nude men selling peanuts" or
"Railway song swims ashore".
How can any mortal
be responsible for these.

2003.

#46.   IF.

If a man
finds a stone on the road and said
"…a diamond fell into my hand today".
Who should comment,
or even care.
A poet would probably say the same.
Listening to those words
I began thinking poetry,
and believed everything.

2003.

#47. LANGUAGE.

The birth of language
a thing divine,
but the word I used
was not mine.
Something fell from the sky
I said rain, looking
for my word in vain.
While studying the world
all around, bright new words
came to my tongue.
Great joy yet despair
filled my mind
of legions of words yet
I had to find.
Whatever I see now
will forever stay,
until real words arrive
to drive them away.

2003.

#48.   WORD-WORLD.

Go put a book on your head
let words become hairstyles.
Others will take serious notice
creating nations of word-heads,
no need to speak just read a head.

Pillows will replace dreams
with words in shimmering syntax.
Cosmetologists seeing themselves
as word-style specialists.
Paintings and sculpture
will be banished from museum halls,
razors, combs and shampoo sprays
taking pride of place.
Relay racers will pass sentences
from ear to waiting ear,
festivals presenting garlands of words.
Guns will fire salvoes of exhortations,
the world itself becoming a word.

2003.

#49.   PLAY.

From here to there
life's chequer-board
of immutable moves.

Open the play
to new insights,
as new leaves
old branch,
new poems
old pages.

2003.

#50.   GO MAD.

"Go mad !"
my friend the poet said.
"Go mad at least once".

Action is not the prerogative only
of gods we cannot see.
We need the rum-of- knowing,
or freedom, like a nestling
challenging flight on supportive wind.

Let madness come
singing all the poems
we want to remember,
that glorious advent of visions
becoming friends.

2004.

#51

62

#51.   AIR AND WORDS.

Words saturate air.
We give them meaning
and like the wind
meanings change.
The word life
presents a conundrum,
confuses philosophers
and writers of tremendous books.

Words like shadows
will remain with us until
the sun itself is a shadow.

2004.

#52.   POEMS AND I.

Will poems ever cease
to be concerned with "I",
although someone said
"Man is not the centre of the universe".
Self is always at the centre
of things we seem to know,
yet knows not itself.

Despite many poems
I do not understand
why visions need words
and words so many poems.
I can however see
why self as conscious "I"
always need help
from patient poems.

2004.

#53.   WINE AND FLOWERS.

In a strange moment surrounded
by tables of wine and flowers
I hear myself speak spark-words.
It is the time of personal echoes.

Poems must be born this way
the magic sounds of words incarnate,
gods walking the earth, poet as seer.
We can become human.

2004.

#54.   THE WORD.

With slight distinction,
vision and concept reside
in infinite space.
How often we wish to hear
conversation between leaf and falling,
between tongue and speaking.

Must I imagine some world
where words have thoughts
about imagined words,
where dictionaries become houses
and libraries cities.
To imagine as well
the poet's declaration,
one breath,
one word.

2004.

#55.   POEMS WITHOUT WORDS.

Piece of string on the floor
playing with crevices,
cat dreaming of
more important things
and I of the impossible.
Shadows speaking
of birds on the moon
and poems without words.

2004.

#56.   BLESS ME.

To worship things from afar,
the Pyramids as eternity,
a sudden face in a crowd
becoming the beloved.

Those poems from Persia
and lines my friend wrote
also blessings in my heart
no 'scope can reach.
Will such worship ever bless me
with things more tangible than
what rushes through my fingers
faster than events in a dream.

2004.

#57.   ANCHORS.

The song is the thing
as any bird knows.
Texture of poetry thus
teases the soul, into realms
where words fall, like mute anchors
from the poems-ship.

2004.

#58. BIRTH OF VISIONS.

Visions are born whole,
with unimpeachable certitude
dissolving the shell of being.

Understanding confers epiphanies
Expanding, like ripples across a pool
until the next revelation.
Visions can be friendly
or dressed in monstrous form
heading for the soul's open door.
This so evident, and yet
remaining in that state,
we wait for whatever comes
in whatever dress.

2004.

#59. "I" THE POEM.

I have become a poem
dressed in words,
talking among themselves.
I listened then to rhymes,
similes grown to metaphors,
allusions dancing to many things.

I thought I knew
only angels appeared in visions,
but here now are poems,
angels becoming nothing more
than stories in sleep
when I become a poem.

2005.

#60. ECHO AND RIPPLE.

Words in speech and song
have echoes like a pebble, ripples.
Words for shadow-memories
are elusive monsters living
in the corner of an eye.

Unlike echoes and ripples
soon fading the shadow-memory
consistently repeats itself
like nocturnal notes of the cricket.
The tumbling search continues,
that word naming the shadow-memory.

2005.

#61.   SIGNIFICANCE.

Like a perennial flower
a thought still blooms, about
the significance of things.

How was the first word
recognized as word.
When was that problem
abruptly pushed aside
attempting to describe,
colour-flash of a rare wing or
crystal fear in a child's eye..

These were significances
with poets adding many more,
the love many hearts knew
and mysteries swarming like bees.

Despite basket of words from
devoted probing minds
the question still remains.

2005.

#62.   RETREAT.

From the sound of voices
the shush of waves even
I retreated into silence like
that ant tempting gravity
on a quiet window pane or
solitary feather resting
in the shadow of roots
and wrote that poem.

2005.

#63.   POINTS.

Everywhere, everywhere
within each verbal construct
metaphysical points signal issues
mapping what will be.
Images sometimes escape that tyranny
but like mythological beings
we are fated to roam between
points edges and elusive form,
the persuasions of poetry.

2005.

#64. POEM THING.

Something is here
if I suddenly turn.
But things revealed
need courage to survive them.

I have thought of this thing
imagined manifestations as poems.
If it be revealed in new-to-me form
surprise will not descend
like tropic swift night.

2005.

#65.   LOCATION.

Any transparent experience
like a new found bird
demands a name, and
the form of a poem.

Beyond the compass
came that transparent thing
breathing as I breathe, its presence
a loving membrane between us.

Direction becomes meaningless
the problem is location
of that particular word
in that particular poem.

2005.

#66.   METAPHOR.

I write,
not to show writing is possible
but as a trusting hunter
hoping butterfly words
will be caught as poems.

I write to show,
to show or perhaps fail,
that the ineffable
may be given form
as flying metaphor
in the sky we call soul.

2005.

#67.   DREAM POEM.

Tired though this hand be
it will not cease to write.
Visions always demand new clothes.
There was the time
I saw a poem in a dream.
Awakened by its beauty
I was ready to write.
new words in new clothes.
On the screen of memory however
was the illumined shape
of missing words.
Sad by that loss,
tired though this hand be,
it will not cease to write.

2005.

#68.   RELEVANCE.

Must I live now,
concerns of another age
and solutions of that time.
It would be unwelcome burden,
like witnessing angels
polishing bullets.

Such things I refute,
dedicating poems
to problems of this day
that seem not to sleep
as nesting birds do.

2005.

#69.   LATE FRUIT.

Last word
like late fruit
is end and start of seasons.
Why did late words drop
as out-of-season writing
surprising the poet's pen,
witness ever to attending storms
in moments of securing imagery,
the blood of poems.

2006.

#70.   WHERE DID IT GO.

Where did it go
that febrile apprehension
of an arriving poem
that burnished feeling, splendid
as a fabulous bird.

I sense something,
unmistakable pathos
 once a sunlit stone
lying now in oceanic dark,
a reminder, silent
as that lost poem.

2006.

#71.   SHADOW-WE.

We walk across the earth
like clouds without shadows.
Have you ever seen
the shadow of a wing
or that of a song
imprinted at the bottom of clouds.
Think now,
of shadows living in our hearts
where poems should be.

2006.

#72. FRAGMENTS.

Fragments of houses,
fragments of dreams,
birds not caring who throws seeds.
Everywhere,
thoughts are scattered
like broken leaves.
Behind windows
remnants of sentences dwell
as we sit in fragments of houses
in our fragments of dreams.

2006.

#73.   SKY TO SING.

We brush by one another
like grains of wave-tossed sand
each alone to interior song or poem
as cane-field smoke kills the sun
in sky that needs to sing
in a sky that needs to sing.

In this world comes a child
unblinking, questioning
reminding us of things past
praises to gods secure elsewhere
and the songs we lost
the poems we lost
in a sky that needs to sing
in sky that needs to sing.

2006.

#74

#74.   UNDERSTANDING.

I see intention
in the eyes of the poet,
listened to his words
hardly understanding.
My ignorance easily pardoned
by soft laughter and
procession of emblazoned imagery.

2006.

#75. THE MUSE.

The muse has gone,
the muse has gone,
lines no longer arrive
like moths to a night flower.
Neither forlorn nor amazed,
just thankful for years
when images flowed
into a receptive consciousness
into presumed poems.

It is not a time to mourn,
it is not a time to mourn
though the muse has gone.

2006.

THE POEMS MAN:
STANLEY GREAVES AND STEWART BROWN
IN CONVERSATION
(December 2007, Crusher Site Road, Prospect, Barbados)

STEWART BROWN: I wanted to ask you first of all about your early contact with Martin Carter.

STANLEY GREAVES: My early contact with Martin Carter was of meeting him at art exhibitions held by Burrowes and the Working Peoples' Art Class [E. R. Burrowes formed the group in 1945; the School of Art in Guyana is named after him]. And then because of the way he spoke and the things that he talked about and the way he talked about them I got very interested because I always like meeting people with ideas, people with imagination and people who are very knowledgeable about things. So I was very attracted to going to Martin's at weekends to sit and talk. We'd talk about my work and he'd talk about his work. He'd talk about philosophy, politics, history, whatever – and listening to him of course led me into reading a bit more into writers like Eliot and Yeats – he was very fond of Eliot and Yeats – and that's how it started.

SB: When were these meetings?

SG: This is in the 50s.

SB: He was some years older than you?

SG: He was senior to me by a number of years, yes. [Martin Carter was born in 1927, Stanley Greaves in 1934.]

SB: So you weren't school mates?

SG: No, no, no, he went to the prestigious Queen's College, I attended St. Stanislaus.

SB: I have a sense of Georgetown at that time as being quite rigidly class conscious?

SG: Not really you know. Some people kept to that colonial

hierarchy and practised it but there *was* social mobility, you met people of all sorts. I mean you had this informal thing whereby you could drop by people's homes without needing to phone them in advance. You know it was all 'Come in and have a talk', so there was no discrimination. But of course, as in any situation involving human beings, there would be cliques, so it was a question of what clique you were going to eventually gravitate towards or be invited to join. So certainly I moved with my fellow artists and I spent a lot of time talking with Martin.

SB: We know he had a vision of the role of the writer, indeed a larger idea of the role of the artist, in a place like Guyana...

SG: Well, he had an idea of the role of the *individual* and the moral practice individuals should pursue. He held that very strongly and it didn't matter whether you were an artist, a musician or a road sweeper, whatever it is you do you have to do with a certain moral purpose and authority. And this is something I found quite fascinating and of course I believe that very strongly myself. So it was from him that I began to have glimmerings of the moral responsibility of the artist, that you are responsible for every stroke you make on the canvas, every chip of wood that comes off a carving, you are responsible for that. And so, therefore, the outcome has to show this. What you produce must have *that* authority about it. As well as, of course, one must have the moral courage to stand up for what you believe in. It doesn't matter what's going on.

SB: Yes, that idea of conviction.

SG: Yes, very strong.

SB: Were you writing at this time?

SG: I was writing quite a lot. But I've been writing poems for as long as I have been painting or drawing. I was never really interested in publishing... I mean here and there I would publish. When Rayman Mandal started doing his *Release* magazine at the university [of Guyana] I did publish things in that. That lasted for a few issues until he went to the United States. But I have never really pursued publication much,

I was more interested in just getting the thing done, …a vision, an idea, a notion. The words come to you and you write them down so you can say, 'Ok, maybe I've got something here.' Then, maybe, that becomes a poem in a collection in a few years.

SB: Did you talk to Martin about your writing? I'm trying to get at the evolving artistic relationship between the two of you…

SG: Yes I'd show some things to Martin, indeed I was quite alarmed by what he did to these damn things! He would say, ok, so this is what you've got here, and rearrange things around, shift emphasis, move lines here and there and come up with a structure. But when you looked at what he wrote, that was a Martin Carter poem, nothing to do with me! When I looked at those things and looked back at what I had actually written, it gave me some insight into his thought processes. As a matter of fact it gave me a greater insight into his thought processes than just by reading his poems, because I knew where the thing came from and could see then how he manipulated the material. I got some really astounding things from that. And those were lessons I learnt.

SB: Can you be more precise about that, what was he doing? How did he manipulate the material?

SG: Well let us say that he was entertaining my vision, but he was coming at it from another perspective even though he was using my lines and what have you. Yet by the time he was through with the deconstructing/ reconstructing process it was a different poem. A poem in its own right that had little or nothing to do with my poem.

SB: He obviously respected your work as a painter, did you have a similar relationship with him in terms of your writing? Or was there no distinction?

SG: Well he could see affinities between my writing and the work I was doing as a painter. But a great deal of our conversation would be spent in dealing with things of a metaphysical nature, notions about 'being', and occupying space, etc. Ok, 'being' but where? Location, locus, where are you…?

93

SB: What would be the occasion of these talks?

SG: Well I would just drop round by Martin. No particular idea in mind, just to sit down and talk, you know? It might be about a book I'd just read or a book he's reading. At one stage he was into these Russian poets and was very excited by what they did in their own country and the price they paid. This is where this thing of courage comes into it.

SB: Was that interest in the Russian poets part of his socialist agenda, or was he just drawn to the poetry?

SG: No, it was again coming through his understanding of poetics. Martin wrote a lot of incredible stuff on poetics, which he kept in note form in notebooks and papers scattered around the place. Rupert Roopnaraine has recently been given access to these things and has begun to put them into various categories. Martin's mind moved in several directions at the same time, it's like something from theoretical physics, so his notes are like that. So Rupert has spent several months going through these notes and essays etc. and categorising them – these are linguistics, these are poetics, social commentary, what have you. But much of it is into linguistics, the structure of the word, the place of the word in a statement and all the things you can extrapolate from that. It's just incredible stuff. I remember, sometimes talking with Martin and he would be flying, and I'm finding it very difficult to keep up with his thoughts, so I would just sit and let him carry on. And one day I said to him, 'You know listening to you talk is hard listening; it's really hard. But over the years I've found a way of dealing with it.' He became curious, and I said, 'What I do is, I listen to you talk but I can't always follow your logic, it moves too swiftly for me. You can see it because you are making these leaps and connections.' ('Leaps' was one of his favourite words.) 'But I would just listen and then somewhere along the line you would say something that would make all the things you said previously fall into place.' Martin thought that was a very curious way to deal with it, but it was the only way I *could* deal with it.

SB: So did you regard yourself and Martin as comrades or did you feel that you were in some kind of learning relationship?

SG: Well for me it was very much of a learning relationship, but when we got into what he was doing in poetry and what I was doing in painting, then we were fellow workers in the same struggle.

SB: Was he interested in your responses to his poems?

SG: Some of them yes, the ones where I found a great deal of resonance. I remember a particular poem, 'The Conjunction'*, it's a later poem which encapsulates all of Martin's themes, not only metaphysical issues but also love poems he wrote, political poems, and also ideas about *the word*. As a matter of fact I use that poem in the catalogue notes that accompany a series of paintings I've made called 'Caribbean Metaphysics'.

SB: In what ways does the poem relate to the paintings?

SG: I've always had this feeling – living in the Caribbean – that we have not arrived at a philosophy of our own, and that therefore we have not *defined* the things that matter, in terms of our identity. We have not identified a philosophy that embraces a world picture, a moral picture of ourselves. I always felt that was a kind of lacuna in our existence here in the Caribbean. When Martin and I were both teaching at the University of Guyana we tried to establish a 'General Introduction to Philosophy' course as a compulsory first year unit. We had people like Bill Carr, Joel Benjamin and Rupert Roopnaraine, as well as Martin – all very well read in philosophy and willing to create and teach courses... but the university turned the proposal down. At that stage I said to myself, we are not at a real university and mentally I signed off.

SB: Didn't you and Martin and some others establish a kind of radical alternative seminar group within the university at one point?

SG: It was Martin, myself, Bill Carr, Rayman Mandal and Mike Aarons – another very bright mind. We all wrote poems. So it was the usual thing, we used to meet and discuss poems, talk about topical things, whatever was of interest to us. We used to meet on Sundays at each other's homes, sometimes we'd meet during the week. If we happened to all be on campus then one of our meetings would be in a rum shop off campus. My poem 'Off Campus Training' (published in *Horizons*] is about that. We thought that what we were doing should be done on campus, in a common-room situation. Rooms were not available but Rayman Mandal – whom I called an urban guerilla – he *liberated* a room and we used to meet there. We would be drinking rum still, but out of tea pots and tea cups, for the sake of 'respectability', but everyone knew we were drinking rum. What amazed me was that we would be sitting there discussing these fundamental things and other colleagues would be passing by but none of them – save Jeff Robinson – would come in to find out what we were doing or join in the discussion. Not one of them! Most odd and distressing! Very distressing. To the extent that we decided 'forget about it', and we returned to the rum shop.

SB: Apart from your years as a student overseas you were in Guyana through most of the Burnham years?

SG: Yes, I left in the early 60s and returned in 1968, and then remained there right through. So I was there throughout the Burnham years.

SB: Alongside Martin Carter…

SG: Yes, and all those other guys.

SB: My sense of it is that it was a tough time, one way and another.

SG: Yes it was a tough time, it was that, for all kinds of reasons, ideological reasons. Tough in the sense that you saw people sort of bow down to what was going on, people in positions of responsibility who dared not say 'No' because if they did they were out… and that used to happen.

SB: But there was this artistic community, some kind of intellectual life, despite the hardships…

SG: It was just among a few people, literally a very few people, not enough to create a community or any kind of movement. You had people like Denis Williams, who produced great work, but was not really interested in politics. There were a lot of people like that, intellectuals, not really interested in politics. Those who were joined this party or that party and indulged in the polemics of politics, Rupert (Roopnaraine) was one of those who was a very serious political theorist and activist who formed a political party, along with Walter Rodney.

SB: Where did you sit in that scenario?

SG: My idea of politics was that if you talk once and then you talk twice and nothing is happening, then it is time to do something else. I can't stand endless talking and debating. I do not have, and do not practise either, the 'art of persuasion'. I hate persuading people to do something. I say something and if there isn't a resonance there and I have to persuade you and I have to persuade a resonance in you, I don't see how one can do that. Actually I think it's immoral. Endless arguments and debates, no, I don't take kindly to that.

SB: So the group of people you describe, meeting on Martin's verandah and such like, they weren't talking about politics?

SG: Sometimes, sometimes, if something was going down then we'd say well, you know, this is what's happening but there's nothing we can do except go and create mayhem or whatever. But then we'd get on with other business.

SB: I'm trying to get a sense of the context in which Martin Carter's work was made and your work both as artist and poet...

SG: Well by the 60s, you know, Carter was out of politics. He resigned from the government. He'd been Minister of Information but when I asked him about what was going on he said, 'Those guys, they talking politics but they are not really interested in being *in* politics, and unless that is happening then there is no point in my being around.'

SB: And is that disappointment reflected in his writing? You know there is this theory that you can see 'a process of disillusion' in Carter's work, from the naïve optimism of the early poems, through disappointment with the way politics in Guyana unfolds, to disillusion and even despair in the late poems.

SG: Yes I read that somewhere, I suppose that is so in some ways. But he was not interested in becoming a public figure or leading a public life. He had his own private investigations to pursue, which he did, and which resulted in those magnificent late poems. Poems that are of a totally different order, a different weight, to those poems of the 50s.

SB: Yes, I think that model of a journey from optimism to despair is too simplistic. It's not disillusion is it – that would imply a loss of energy – but it seems to me that there is something else going on, he makes a decision to do *something else*.

SG: Yes, he was writing based on his perception of things and also producing these incredible notes about all kinds of things. And I remember, when the discussions we had got pretty heady, I would go home immediately and try and reconstruct the conversation in my journals.

SB: Yes we should talk about your journals, and the notes that you made are really quite extensive aren't they?

SG: Yes, the notes I made with Carter; I made copies for Gemma Robinson when she was doing her research, and I knew I had this stuff but I was amazed by the amount I'd gathered over the years.

SB: I'm still trying to get a clear sense of your relationship. Did you consider him a friend or a mentor?

SG: Yes, great friend, a mentor, a drinking companion… the whole works. It was all wrapped up in one. You know, things can change depending on what it is we were talking about. Things can change very quickly. So I knew, when the germ of an idea came up and he started running with it, well that was when I became a listener – I wasn't participating except as a listener. To hear what was coming out… the conclusions he was drawing, that fascinated me.

SB: When I first met him, in 1988, after Guyana had been pretty much cut off from the outside world for a while – you couldn't get books, for example, at all easily – what struck me was how up to date he was in terms of his engagement with literary theory and ideas.

SG: Because of his own investigations into linguistics and poetics, he was always curious as to what 'these fellows' – as he used to call them – had come up with, as opposed to what he himself was working on. So he always had an idea of what was going on 'out there'.

SB: Was he much of a correspondent d'you know?

SG: No, Martin was too busy corresponding with himself and his ideas.

SB: We have this idea of him serving as a model of the committed individual, in terms of the role of the artist. I'm wondering to what extent, more specifically, he offered you a model of 'the poet'?

SG: I think my own natural instinct towards metaphysics is what attracted me to his poems, particularly the later poems. Investigation into that kind of world was particularly fascinating to me. That has formed the basis of my writing. I find lyrical poems and narrative poems hard to read – to follow – because for me they are 'descriptions', poetic descriptions and allusions, yes, but for me the poem must be an 'investigation'.

SB: Can you expand on what you mean by 'investigation'?

SG: I mean the poems I have written that are dedicated to Martin – as well as a number of others I have not included in the collection – are dealing with that idea of an investigation into the nature of 'being'. I am not a reader of philosophy as such, what I do is read commentaries, so I have an inkling of who did what and when. But for me the poems are a form of discovery on my own, which may mean reinventing the wheel, but who cares? The whole notion of 'being' is very central to my work in poetry, indeed in all my creative work.

SB: And you credit Carter with inspiring that understanding…?

SG: Yes, helping what was there to emerge, making me realise that maybe I was on to something, and then helping me to sustain it. So staying on the path I had started. But staying on the path did not mean I had to try to emulate what he was doing. Rather it was his example, the way he pursued his own vision, staying on the path to see what he would find.

SB: So was that the motivation for writing this group of poems, to acknowledge that example?

SG: Well yes, as I'm writing the idea would come to me that yes, this looks like a poem to Martin. If you notice the nub of the collection is to do with words and how we use words, which was very much one of Martin's concerns. But I find it fascinating myself, what does a particular word 'mean'?

SB: As a collection, some of the poems are *about* Martin Carter in some way, some of them are concerned with his ideas, others are more loosely related to him. Did you set out to write such a collection or did you realise gradually that you had this set, as it were…

SG: No, I didn't set out to write a book of Martin poems, the first group I wrote were included in my collection *Horizons* but they kept cropping up and cropping up until last year, when I felt I'd reached the last of the poems here, I thought, 'it's time to close this off.' But in fact the ideas explored in these poems are still resonating.

SB: Yes I can see that, in the movement towards the haiku that I know you have been working on, the poems get tighter and shorter – a bit like what happens with Carter's own work over time, it becomes more intense…

SG: Like a nut, a kernel, tighter and tighter.

SB: So to sum up Carter's influence; he's a friend, a mentor, he gives you a model of the individual in the society, in his person and his practice he has given you a model of a kind of poet's life…

SG: Not so much a poet's life, more a commitment to what you are carrying in your mind and if you have a vision then you have to find a way of cultivating it.

SB: No matter the circumstances?

SG: Yes, no matter the circumstances. One of Martin's favourite words was 'proceed'.

SB: I keep harping on about the difficult circumstances because of the way Carter stayed in Guyana through those difficult times, when he could easily have migrated to more comfortable situations overseas.

SG: Yes but Martin was not interested in 'recognition', or his literary reputation in those terms. Many of his later poems were written on scraps of paper and what-have-you, left all over the place and just discarded. They were actually 'rescued', picked up and collected by Rayman Mandal (who published *Poems of Affinity* in 1980) because – unlike me – Martin was not the kind of person who needs to put things neatly into a book or journal so that he could find them. I think Martin regarded the making of his poems as a natural process, like breathing, just part of him. You don't think about collecting your breaths, you just breathe, so Martin would just breathe a poem out and let it go. He felt a strong affinity with the Chinese poet Li Po, who had a similar attitude.

SB: How would he have known about Li Po?

SG: Martin was extremely widely read. Friends of his would bring books back when they travelled out. People would bring in magazines etc. So it was like the world came to him rather than him going to the world. And he would see something going on there and he would make a note of it. He definitely wasn't interested in university life, campus and going about the place as 'the poet', he was too busy.

SB: Too busy with his 'investigations'?

SG: Yes, of course. And there is much of that in the ways I work as well. I am so busy doing stuff I can't be bothered going about organising exhibitions, getting my stuff published in books and all that. Too busy with the actual 'work', you know, the actual work is the important thing. I have this image of myself like a medieval monk, you know, who is in a little cubby hole somewhere and writing all kinds of abstruse things – angels on pins and all kinda stuff like that.

A man who can't be bothered with what's going on outside because this, the work you are doing, is what IS. Is what IS. That's my anchor, it's everything.

SB: Would you say that is the fundamental attitude that you shared with Martin?

SG: Yes, I shared the same view. I wouldn't say it was something I necessarily learned from him, it was more a recognition within myself, that this thing exists here and I need to do something about it.

SB: But Martin Carter's decision to stay on in Guyana was partly political commitment, wasn't it?

SG: No I don't think so. I don't think the possibility of working in universities and travelling around the metropolitan centres was something that particularly excited him. It didn't pull him. I remember he very reluctantly went and spent that year in England, at the University of Essex, but he went very reluctantly. He felt it was a distraction.

SB: And did that attitude continue until the end of his life? You were around after he had his stroke weren't you?

SG: Yes. I do remember after he had his stroke what a thing that was because he could no longer write, and I remember asking him one day, 'Are you writing still?' and he said, 'No, I know I have things inside me, but I am watching how I am trying to retrieve what I know is inside there.' He never succeeded, the stroke destroyed him. He literally had to learn to write again, how to hold a pen. It was very distressing. I went by his house once when he was just setting off for a therapy session and he asked if I would come with him, to keep him company. Of course I said yes. I wanted to see what this therapy was about too. The therapist gave him a ballpoint pen and a sheet of paper and said to him, 'Ok Martin, think of a sentence and then copy it down.' He had to get back how to manipulate a pen. But he just sat there and he said to me, rapping the pen on the table, 'Give me a sentence, give me a sentence.' Martin Carter is asking me to give him a sentence. That told me the extent to which his mind had been damaged. I was quite surprised and appalled.

SB: Getting back to Martin's influence on your practice as a poet, can you say more about what you took from him in terms of his use of language.

SG: Accuracy: the word and its place. When you use a word be very aware of its 'location'. And also of the things that you can extrapolate from that word in that location. And if you put it in another location what happens to that word, is it still the same word? I think I did a poem about that.

SB: Yes you have a poem called 'Word' in the middle of the collection, indeed there are several on that linguistic theme…

SG: Yes, there's another one where I talk about reading a book and having a drink of rum at the same time, then waking up in the morning and finding the book and the rum there and wondering if it was the same rum and the same book…

SB: Those are kind of philosophical speculations…

SG: Well yes you see that was what made me want to have philosophy at the university. The least we can do is to create a situation where people can speculate in a very serious manner – not that idle speculation idea – because on the back of that speculation comes action. Action comes afterward. I feel that we have not established that tradition of speculative thought, it's not there. We have academic thought but speculative thought, no. But that's where Martin's work and his whole being was so located because he was always speculating about things. What does this thing mean? And because I am extremely visual, you know, I transfer that into my own work. I see something and I question, what is that thing doing *there*? Location. And what is the meaning or significance that can be derived from that? So in my mini paintings, the 'Caribbean Metaphysics' series I mentioned earlier, what I wanted to do was to begin this action of speculation by saying, ok, the first things we have to speculate about are the things that are around us and the relationships among them. And perhaps when we can deal with that we can think about *events*, and the relationships between events. Then, ultimately, we can speculate about ourselves. The most fundamental speculations are about ourselves: the essence of self. But we don't have it and I think that absence is a great loss.

SB: In what ways particularly?

SG: In the Caribbean we talk so much about identity but unless we engage in certain kinds of speculation we are not getting anywhere. As a matter of fact at this point in time I'm not sure that the notion of identity has any relevance really. When you consider how fragmented the world has become today.

SB: Go on…

SG: Well when you consider that so many artists of the Caribbean are living outside of the region and then they have these big problems of identity… I don't see the big problem, your identity is to deal with the things that are around you, the basic things that are around you. If I was living somewhere, and this was where I was going to live, then my eyes would be out there, looking at what was around me to see what was resonating for me, not looking back to the Caribbean. I have to deal with what is in front of me.

SB: So like Grace Nichols' poem, 'wherever I hang my knickers/ that's my home…'?

SG: I had an exhibition in London and a woman came up and asked me 'Why are you still in the Caribbean, why are you not here?' I said, well, because I like to be where I can see certain things, the things that interest ME. But it doesn't matter where I go I would find things that would interest me – for example I picked up on some dolls on a recent trip which feed into the doll paintings I've been doing. It doesn't matter where I go I will see things that create a resonance and then I use it. I know that you can carry your environment in your mind and people get into that whole nostalgia trip, but there are certain things you cannot carry and when you have to go into a new environment well then you use past experience to help you to deal with that new situation.

SB: You are bound to carry your own past with you to some extent and to see through the eyes that past has somehow formed...

SG: Of course, you carry your own baggage, you can't help that. It's like when I was a student at Howard University and all this Black Power thing was going on, my reaction was, when they were talking about blackness, I said, well, I have a big problem because the person who is now talking to you is both slave and slave master, so I don't know whose side to take! You could have heard the proverbial pin drop! And I said, you know, I do not accept other people's definition of myself, *I* define me. If *you* allow yourself to be defined by other people and you act by that definition, well, that's your problem, not mine.

SB: Yes well that kind of stuff goes around and around. I was talking to my UWI students here about it the other day, and – you know the Brathwaite/Walcott divide – where, crudely, the choice is between Caribbean history as a burden of injustice as against the notion of 'the spoils of history', New World history as a treasure trove that as a West Indian person you can draw what you want from and reject other elements... The response seems to be a kind of temperamental thing... some people want – or need – to focus on the injustices, others want to – and it's not about forgiving or forgetting – but finding ways to move on...

SG: Yes, just seeing it, identifying it and moving on. This moving on business, it's like one day I was in a shop and I saw a little Chinese wooden carving of a Buddha. The Buddha was laughing. I thought this is a paradox – why is he laughing? I came to the conclusion that the Buddha was himself acknowledging the paradox, that when you are in the face of a paradox you are facing truth. I decided that the Buddha was laughing because that's what you do when you confront a paradox; recognise it, bow, laugh and go along your way. The essence of my thinking is around the idea of paradox. What a wonderful thing a paradox is, how it can make you feel very uncomfortable just because there are no answers coming out of it.

SB: Yes that links in very well with the riddling quality of some of your work, which we can come back to I hope. But staying with this idea of words and investigating and interrogating words. Can we just look at the at poem of yours, 'Word', number 16 in the collection. Can you talk me through it? What's going on in that poem?

SG: Ok. Well in many of these poems it's the first two or three lines that come to me first and then as I write them down the rest of the poem begins to reveal itself. 'It is the time of thread and spade'; somehow or another, it's like coming to the end of something. It's time to get rid of it, it's time to bury it. You have to measure a body, you measure a body and then use the spade to dig the grave.

SB: The image of the thread and spade is very clever. But I wonder how many people reading that would pick up on the idea of the shroud and the measuring up of the body...?

SG: Oh do you think so? I think it's there, if you read on, if you are lost with the 'thread and spade' then you come to 'buried', that takes you back to the associations of those words.

SB: Yes, once you say it, it seems obvious and quite clear, and you leave us enough clues elsewhere in the poem.

SG: ...*time to measure useless words* [Puts emphasis on 'useless words']
and bury them in the wind.
Don't hold on to them, just loose them like a kite, let them fly away like dead leaves, bury them in the wind.
From every ancient trunk and cavern
visions will be extracted...
That's where you have to look – the reception or extraction – I use extraction but it's really reception – of visions.
...Flawed concepts
however confined in world-of-books
discarded like cracked bricks.
People tend to follow the book. They will read something in a book and as far as they are concerned, that's it, a book is not to be questioned. But a book for me is a conversation. You can always tell a book that I have read because there are all these notes in the margins. And I am always vexed that publishers don't leave a wide enough space of blank paper! So I have this very fine pen that I write

with in the margins of all my books. So…

> Flawed concepts
> however confined in world-of-books
> (must be) *discarded like cracked bricks.*

SB: In your version, have you got 'must be' in the last line there?

SG: I have it, but I crossed it out…

SB: In the corrected version you sent me those words are omitted. One of the things I'm interested in is how you make those decisions, about what to change, what to leave alone.

SG: Yes, the lines should read:

> *However confined in world-of-books*
> *discarded like cracked bricks*
> *Always the poet must taste*
> *fine rum* [aside: 'That's Martin']
> *and (the) sound of each constructed syllable*
> [aside: 'That's Martin again.']
> *as dress of poems*

SB: Although in the poem it is laid out as the one piece, there are three or four ideas being explored here. And in terms of the process we have been talking about, paring down your words, you have taken away, in some sense, the obvious linkages, so the poem has to be almost 'reconstructed' by the reader to restore those connections. You are asking the reader to do some extra work. How do you come to those decisions?

SG: Because I see those 'buffer words' as preventing you from getting to the core of the poem. It's connections again. If I don't see those connections really functioning then I just take them out. They must be *necessary*, they must really be vital to the poem or otherwise I just chop them out.

SB: And is that approach something you took from Martin Carter? Is that something he would have approved of?

SG: Oh yes, the concision of line and image is what I learned from him. Also, as we went on, because of the way that Martin carried on a dialogue or a discussion, his way of dealing with words and the meanings of words, investigating all of the kinds of nuances and innuendos you can get from words, particular words depending on the context. I was very stimulated by this and it has continued to inspire me in what I do, especially in the written word. Ambiguities – forget about it – redundancies and tautologies... no no no... you have to get to the kernel of the matter and express it in as concise a way as possible.

SB: Yes, there is a kind of lean, clipped precision about the language of these poems...

SG: All these flowery words and phrases rambling on, as I said, after a while I learned to distrust adjectives and adverbs... They are the kinds of things that get people into trouble.

SB: But they are also, in a sense, the 'oil' of prose aren't they...

SG: Yes they are the oil of prose, yes, but I find I tend to like the poetic way they are used in imagery by Latin American writers, just the poetry of it, the mosaic, things coming to you in a pattern like that rather than in a straight line. I like that.

SB: I hear what you say. Indeed I feel like that about Wilson Harris, I read his fiction as if it were poetry as I don't pick up enough of the references to read them as linear narratives. But if I read them as long sequences of connected prose poems, then...

SG: That makes sense...

SB: No, it doesn't make sense! But it makes it possible for me to read them, to find a way into them. But to push a bit harder at your reading of 'Word'. You say you got the first three lines and then the poem grows from there?

SG: In this particular poem I think it was the first line that came to me, this line just came to me – 'It is the time of thread and spade'. And then the rest of it just followed from there.

SB: How do you come to the title, 'Word'?

SG: Its about words, you know the sound of each constructed syllable, Word, the dress of poems. Words, concepts that you find in books, useless words, throw them away.

SB: '*The* dress of poems'? When you read it earlier you said 'as dress of poems'?

SG: Yes, that was right. "The dress" doesn't make any sense. It should be 'as dress of poems', because it is all poems, 'the dress' makes it too particular.

SB: Also, as you have it now, '*each constructed syllable/as dress of poems*' opens up the possibility of another meaning; dress as in masonry, you know, to dress stone, to shape it and give it a public face.

SG: Well that's a possibility I hadn't thought about, but as I meant it the syllables will construct the dress, so the syllables as dress 'becomes' the poem. So all the syllables together become the dress, so the syllables as dress *is* the poem.

SB: Yes I see, becomes in a sense the fabric of the poem.

SG: Yes.

SB: I chose to look closely at that poem 'Word' not only because it focuses on this central concern of the collection, with words and the making of poetry, but also because it is among a group of poems that are very reminiscent of Martin's later work.

SG: Yes other people have commented on this, in a rather critical way. It has been suggested that this is a negative thing. But I feel that Carter's heroes in poetry were people were like Eliot and Yeats, especially Yeats. And it was not that he was setting out to model his work on theirs but rather that he regarded them as moral persons who were doing certain things with conviction and a certain 'rightness' (that was another of his words, rightness). And he wanted to emulate that 'rightness' in his own work in Guyana. He had no option really but to look outside of the region for his models. So I feel that I am living in the Caribbean and here is a great poet whose work I understand to a degree and whose particular way of writing I find resonates with me.

I find myself writing in that way but I'm not setting out to copy him. And I see no reason why I shouldn't do that, and if it is recognised that I am doing that well 'Hurray!' That's my model. And hey, *I* don't have to look outside of the Caribbean for a model.

SB: My sense of Carter is that he had that attitude as well. Indeed that actually most of the great poets have had it, that they are not interested in those kinds of artificial political boundaries that restrict their entitlement to be open to the writing of the world. Walcott has this idea of a great community of writers, of the past and the present, living wherever they were or are, all being in a pot together, and that they are all engaged in a kind of poetry workshop, listening to each other, critiquing each other's things, taking what they need, you then go and make your own poem, you are not copying anybody, it's the process of being part of this community of poets...

SG: Yes, being part of that community, yes, you see a certain kind of imagery coming up and you say yes, that's my kind of imagery. What I feel is a *confirmation*, you are confirming your locus, of where you are, that's what you are doing. I like reading the work of the Latin American poets because I feel they are all Imagists, you know from out of the French school (I remember when I first read Rimbaud, a wonderful book, Penguin, which I picked up in Trinidad on my way to Britain, on a boat. So I had ten days with Rimbaud – man that thing really blew my mind because of the way the guy was using imagery, putting things in these strange conjunctions, the imagination, the drawing of the images – it really fascinated me, and I said yes, this is the way to write.) So anyway, I got caught on the French Imagists as my model and the Latin American poets who are firmly entrenched in that particular tradition.

SB: Yes I think it makes much more sense to read Martin Carter in the Latin American tradition alongside Octavio Paz, Neruda, César Vallejo...

SG: Yes I remember when Rayman Mandal introduced us to Cesar Vallejo, man, we all got drunk that day! Metaphorically I should say, got drunk on his singing, stuff that we could feel and sense and he was saying it with such conviction. So to this day every now and again I pick up my edition of Vallejo, and I look through it and it's one of those bilingual editions so I can really compare and contrast... with my great knowledge of Spanish where I got up to page 27 in *Teach Yourself Spanish*, haha...

SB: So we have talked about your influences and your ambition as a poet; can I ask about your idea of an audience, who do you envisage as your readers?

SG: I never really paid any attention to who, specifically, is going to be reading these things. My hope is that whoever is reading them understands the nature of words and therefore can move in between the words as I have written them, and extract a meaning that makes sense, makes sense to them. I think it is very difficult – for me at least – to try to direct a particular construct, whatever it is, whatever form, to an audience. You have to follow the dictates of what the construct needs and of your particular vision. You just put the thing out there – it's like fishing – and see what response you get. You can always be surprised. I was once collared by an old grandmother, in the 1972 CARIFESTA, she came into my exhibition and she saw a collage I had done about Jung. She wanted to know who he was. I said he was a man who deals with dreams, and one hour later we were still talking. So I don't know if it's so much a matter of education or a matter of perception, but of course education helps. But I think if the raw material of perception is there then as you read you will be able to find stuff that is relevant to you and your experiences. Or you may find that you can share in an experience that you have never had but you can share in it because of the way it is presented.

SB: Some poets would find that idea, that the reader finds their own poem, and it's not necessarily the poem that the poet set out to provide, problematic.

SG: I don't think you can escape that. No. The nature of words prevents that 'fixed' meaning. The nature of words supports the fact that other people will read their poems in yours. I don't think that is a negative thing, I think it's a human thing – it's inescapable. In fact if you don't allow that then you are treating the reader as a bloody robot, just a receiver. You have to allow that people are going to see a poem in another light, are going to examine it, twist it around – like how you look at a ripe mango, you turn it around, up and down. No, I think it is inevitable, even you might say a necessary thing, that people will read their own poem into your words, it allows them in as participants in the making of poetry.

SB: I suppose it's always a process of negotiation, reading a poem, something that the poet was trying to say and you are trying to find what that was but you are also, as you say, inevitably writing/ reading your own poem.

SG: I know when I read Seamus Heaney for example, I am seeing things there and I am reading a certain amount but I am sure there are other things in there that I am not seeing. For me it's a question too of culture because I am not of that culture there will be certain references and things I will not pick up on. There was one of his I did like especially about a small boy playing hopscotch or marbles or something and I think I was able to get everything out of that because when I was a small boy I liked to play marbles on the street and draw lines to play hopscotch. But many other things, no, I don't have the tools to relate to. And I don't have a problem with that.

SB: But you are someone who is interested in form…

SG: Oh yes I am a Formalist, a thing must have a form if it is to be a 'thing'. So I am very conscious of construction, of form, of the shape of things.

SB: But your poems are not traditionally patterned as verse, are they?

SG: No they are not, they're not. I think Bill Carr, who has written on my poetry, once remarked that the poems were shaped by 'the rhythm of speaking, not the metric foot.' I liked that.

SB: How do you test the form then? Do you read them aloud, or in your head?

SG: Well after writing and looking at drafts and editing and looking at it as a written thing, then I start reading it to myself and that's when some of these words start dropping out.

SB: So the test is aural?

SB: Yes, the test is aural. Oh yes. That's what tells me that certain lines are wrong. Maybe when I wrote the line down the words run out but when I speak it I say no, that doesn't work, you have to stop that. So the declaiming to yourself is *extremely* important. For me that is how the rhythm of my poems is determined. In the first instance, in the writing there is a certain amount of shaping but then in the final analysis it is the hearing of it that really determines the form.

SB: Did you talk to Martin about such things?

SG: We did talk about poetry being fundamentally verbal and not written. We actually talked very little about 'our' poems. No. We really talked more about the nature of poetry, the act of writing a poem. What it is. From my experience I came to the conclusion that I am being written by the poems. By which I mean that I can't come in here and see these Christmas lights and think ok, I'll write a poem about fairy lights. Or at least I can do that, but I am so highly conscious of the 'exercise' that it loses something. And perhaps to that extent I am not a true poet.

SB: Quite the opposite, I'd say.

*Martin Carter

THE CONJUNCTION

Very sudden is the sought conjunction.
Sought once over and found once over
and again, in the same sudden place.

It is where the hair grows.
It is where the hand goes.
It is the conjunction
of loin and the rare
possibility of a head
on the cushion of hair and love.

Indeed, I have always wanted
to climb upon a window sill
to climb and compete with the rain
falling down, and rising up.
And staying still, in the promissory
hope of passion's signature
and the returned wealth of a conjunction.

ABOUT THE AUTHOR

Stanley Greaves was born in Guyana. He studied Art in Guyana under E.R. Burrowes, in the UK and the USA as a Fulbright Fellow. He was head of the Division of Creative Arts at the University of Guyana for several years. He left Guyana in 1987 and has been resident in Barbados since that time. He is one of the Caribbean's most distinguished artists with major exhibitions in the UK (The Elders, with Brother Everald Brown) and Europe as well as throughout the Caribbean. In addition to his poetry and art work in several disciplines, he is also a dedicated student of the classical guitar.

ALSO BY AND ABOUT STANLEY GREAVES

Stanley Greaves
Horizons
ISBN: 9781900715577;pp. 152; pub. 2002; £9.99

Stanley Greaves brings a painter's perceptions and a musician's ear to the writing of this substantial selection of his poetry written over the past forty years. He describes his painting as 'a kind of allegorical story-telling' and the same kind of connections between the concrete and the metaphysical, and the presence of the extraordinary in the ordinary are found in his poems.

Greaves guesses at a background that includes African, Amerindian and European ancestry, but declines to relate to any of these in an exclusive way. Rather he writes out of a creole sensibility that celebrates Guyanese diversity: Afro-Guyanese folkways, Amerindian legend and Hindu philosophy. Nor does he reject Europe, and in his poetry and his painting explores connections between European Surrealism and the intuitive elements within Guyana's heterogeneous culture.

To enter the collection is to discover a whole, self-created world of Blakean richness, one which is never static, but growing to encompass new elements. Greaves's is a dialectical vision, alert both to the movements of history and the minutiae of daily change.

His themes include family, daily life, metaphysical speculation, the hard years of social collapse and political repression in Guyana, the strange visitations of inner imaginative life and his comradeship with the great Guyanese poet Martin Carter. His is a sensibility 'welcoming as the earth is/ for every floating seed/ on stairs of air and rain'.

This collection won the 2002 Guyana Prize for the best first collection of poetry.

Rupert Roopnaraine
The Primacy of the Eye
ISBN: 9781900715867; pp. 224; pub. 2005; £16.99

Stanley Greaves is without question one of the Caribbean's most distinguished artists and this critical monograph is both a long overdue investigation and appreciation of his work and an important contribution to the still small body of Caribbean writing about art. Roopnaraine's approach takes as its starting point Greaves' own reference to 'the primacy of the eye as a means of defining fundamentals of a Caribbean experience that cuts through or transcends the history of colonialism'. Roopnaraine's is in the first place an exploration of Stanley Greaves' highly original visual language, but one which draws attention to the significance of Greaves' practice in bringing together elements from visual resources that range across traditional African and Amerindian art and contemporary European surrealism. Again, whilst this is in the first place a description and analysis of the visual and the importance for Greaves of the physical materials he works in, Roopnaraine never loses sight of the fact that Greaves is a Guyanese artist with explicit, though never overdetermining cultural and political concerns.

Chapters explore the roots of Greaves' art in Guyanese physical reality ('If all other records of modern Guyanese life were to disappear, a study of Greaves' paintings of compassion of the fifties and sixties would be enough to tell us how we lived...'); his work in sculpture and ceramics; the impact of his explorations of the bush of the Guyanese interior and a move into more abstract spacial concerns; his return to figure paintings and an extensive investigation of the folk resources of Caribbean art; his visual response to the desolate years of political dictatorship and social collapse in the Guyana of the 1980s in a more explicitly 'readable' art; and the art of his more recent years of inner exploration and what has been described as a Caribbean metaphysic.

The book is illustrated with 78 full colour images of Greaves' paintings, sculptures and ceramics and black and white illustrations from his notebooks.

Laurence Lieberman
Hour of the Mango Black Moon
ISBN: 9781900715935; pp. 120; pub. 2004; £12.99

'We began by speaking in our own voices and tongues/ then other voices/ might take possession of our throats, our/ Souls, for however brief or prolonged a moment'. These lines describing the inner world of Stanley Greaves' painting, 'Morning Mangoes' also describe the intensity and inwardness of Laurence Lieberman's meeting with the paintings of Greaves and two others of the Caribbean's visionary masters, Ras Akyem and Ras Ishi. In their language and reference, these poems are utterly contemporary, but gain resonance from being part of a poetic tradition of 'pictorialism' that perhaps reached its height in the 19th century with Browning and Ruskin's poetic prose.

To label these poems as 'descriptions' of the thirty or so paintings focused on in this collection gives no hint of their multiple rewards. They begin, indeed, in the kind of description found only in the very best art criticism: infectiously enthusiastic, exact, clear in the distinction between observation and speculation. They create rewarding and very human connections between the paintings and their makers. We meet them as vivid characters – Greaves with his oblique charm, Akyem's combative, restless energy, Ishi's elusive, enigmatic intensity – and Lieberman finds acutely appropriate and different dramatic styles to represent each painter and their work. But these poems are not merely commentaries on paintings but meditations that begin in the encounter with the art work and grow from that point. Above all, these are poems that work as poems in finding the language and architecture to capture the moment of engagement with the paintings in all its mixture of exactness and provisionality. The collection is illustrated with sixteen colour plates of paintings described in the book.

All Peepal Tree titles are available from the website
www.peepaltreepress.com
with a money back guarantee, secure credit card ordering
and fast delivery throughout the world at cost or less.